Yellow Umbrella Books are published by Capstone Press
151 Good Counsel Drive, P.O. Box 669, Mankato, Minnesota 56002
http://www.capstone-press.com

Library of Congress Cataloging-in-Publication Data
Christian, Eleanor.
  Let's make butter/by Eleanor Christian and Lyzz Roth-Singer.
  p. cm.
  Includes index.
  ISBN 0-7368-0728-4
  1. Butter—Juvenile literature. [1. Butter.] I. Roth-Singer, Lyzz. II. Title.
SF263.C64 2001
637'.2—dc21
                                                              00-036475

Summary: Describes the ways food can change, using butter as an example, and shows the steps needed to make heavy cream into butter.

Editorial Credits:
Susan Evento, Managing Editor/Product Development; Elizabeth Jaffe, Senior Editor;
  Charles Hunt, Designer; Kimberly Danger and Heidi Schoof, Photo Researchers

Photo Credits:
All photos by Ken Lax except pages 8-9: International Stock/Nancy Wasserman

1 2 3 4 5 6 06 05 04 03 02 01

Let's Make Butter

By Eleanor Christian and Lyzz Roth-Singer

Consulting Editor: Gail Saunders-Smith, Ph.D.
Consultants: Claudine Jellison and Patricia Williams
Reading Recovery Teachers
Content Consultant: Vivian O'Dell,
Staff Scientist at Fermi National Accelerator Lab

Yellow Umbrella Books

an imprint of Capstone Press
Mankato, Minnesota

Foods can change
in many ways.

Have you eaten ice cream
on a sunny day?
If you don't eat quickly,
it melts away.

What about ice cubes that keep things cold?

They melt into water that is hard to hold.

4

Now let's make butter.
We will watch other ways
foods change.

You can turn cream
that you can pour into butter
that you can spread.

Do you know where
butter comes from?

Butter comes from cream.
Cream comes from milk.
Milk comes from cows.

To make butter, you will need a measuring cup, heavy cream, and a jar with a lid.

Have someone work with you at school or at home.

Here are the steps you
need to do.

Measure 1 cup
of cream.

Pour the
cream into
a 2-cup
jar.

Close the
lid tightly.

Now shake, shake.

Shake the jar hard.
Shake it some more.
Shake, SHAKE, **SHAKE**
like you did before.

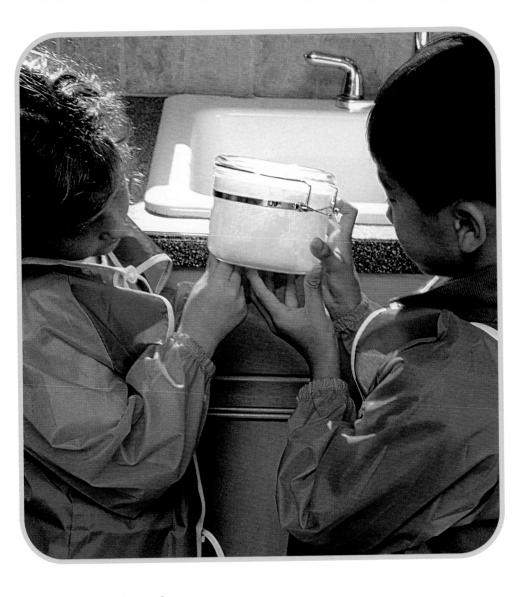

Watch the cream.
How does it change?

Most of the cream becomes
a yellow solid.
That yellow solid is butter.

Any liquid left in the jar
is buttermilk.
Pour out the buttermilk
and put the butter in a bowl.

Now that the cream is butter,
you can spread it on crackers.
You can add jelly.
You can eat it for a snack.

Here is what we did to make butter.

1

Measure 1 cup of cream.

2

Pour cream into jar.

3

Close lid tightly.

4

Shake, SHAKE, SHAKE!

5

Shake until cream turns into butter.

6

Pour out buttermilk.

7

Put butter in a bowl.

8

Eat and enjoy!

Words to Know/Index

butter—the yellow fat made from cream; pages 5, 6, 8, 13, 14, 15, 16

buttermilk—the sour liquid that is left after butter is made from cream; pages 14, 16

change—to become different; pages 2, 5, 12

cream—a thick liquid found in milk; cream can be made into butter; pages 5, 6, 8, 9, 12, 13, 15, 16

liquid—something wet that flows freely; page 14

measure—to find out the exact size or weight of something; pages 9, 16

measuring cup—a tool used to find the exact amount of a liquid; page 8

melt—to change from a solid to a liquid by warming up; pages 3, 4

pour—to make something flow in a steady stream; page 5, 14, 16

snack—a small, light meal; page 15

solid—something that holds its shape; page 13

spread—to cover a surface with something; page 5, 15

2-cup jar—a container that can hold at least 2 cups of something; page 9

Word Count: 223
Early-Intervention Levels: 9–12